THE

CHURCH EXTENSION COMMITTEE

OF THE

General Assembly.

CONSTITUTION, PRINCIPLES, RULES AND ADDRESS.

PHILADELPHIA:
PUBLISHED BY THE COMMITTEE.
PRINTED BY HENRY B. ASHMEAD.
1855.

CHURCH EXTENSION COMMITTEE.

REV. ALBERT BARNES,
REV. THOMAS J. SHEPHERD,
REV. BENJ. J. WALLACE,
JOHN A. BROWN, ESQ.,
GEORGE L. PRENTISS, D. D.,
SAMUEL T. SPEAR, D. D.,
HON. JOHN L. MASON,
THOMAS BRAINERD, D. D.,
REV. HENRY DARLING,
MATTHEW W. BALDWIN, ESQ.,
THOMAS P. SPARHAWK, ESQ.,
JONATHAN F. STEARNS, D. D.,
JOHN C. SMITH, D. D.,
JOSEPH B. SHEFFIELD, ESQ.,
HON. EDWARD A. LAMBERT.

REV. ALBERT BARNES, *Chairman.*
REV. BENJ. J. WALLACE, *Secretary Pro. Tem.*
B. B. COMEGYS, ESQ., *Treasurer Pro. Tem.*
Philadelphia Bank.

☞ Communications for the Committee may be addressed to the Chairman, or Secretary *Pro. Tem.* Donations to the Treasurer, or any of the Officers.

ACTION OF THE GENERAL ASSEMBLY.

The Committee on Church Extension to whom were referred the Overtures and Memorials on the subject of Home Missions, from the Third and Fourth Presbyteries of Philadelphia, the Synod of Iowa, and the Presbyteries of Chicago and Iowa City, respectfully report: That their attention has been especially directed to those cases of home missionary effort, which are excluded by the rules of the American Home Missionary Society. Such are, for example, the employment of Synodical, Presbyterial, and generally of exploring or itinerant Presbyterian missionaries, and the planting of Presbyterian churches in advance of all others in towns and neighborhoods, and the founding of churches within the chartered limits of cities and large villages.

The Form of Government of our Church, chapter XVIII, expressly authorizes the inferior judicatories to apply to the General Assembly for missionary assistance, and in express terms authorizes the Assembly to send missionaries to any part of the Church. The principles of our Presbyterianism, applicable to this subject are, that the Church is one; that, in accordance with this idea, the stronger parts of the Church must assist the weaker, and that the reservoir into which the surplus shall flow to be equalized and distributed, is the General Assembly. It is obvious that the details of the reception and distribution of funds for this object cannot be arranged by the whole body of the Assembly, but that the Assembly must employ some agency for this purpose; and our opinion is that it is entirely free to choose any agency whatever. Of course it may operate through a voluntary association like the American Home Missionary Society; but your Committee do not conceive that its use of that Society for specific purposes either gives that Society a right to control the whole subject of Church Extension for our denomination, or releases the General Assembly from its own obligation to do so. The older and richer Synods, indeed, do not feel so much the pressure of this necessity, as they are able to afford the needed supplementary aid from their own resources; but it is urged upon us from the more new and destitute portions of our Church, that our interests are grievously suffering, because neither the American Home Missionary Society nor any other agency meets their wants in certain respects, such as those which have been already mentioned; and their appeal in this behalf is made just where the Constitution of our Church directs that it should be made—to the General Assembly itself.

This being obviously, therefore, a case which cannot be reached so effectually by any action of the inferior judicatories, your Committee cannot see how the Assembly can refuse to exercise, in regard to it, that power of "superintendence of the concerns of the whole Church," expressly confided to it by the Constitution. They therefore recommend the following action:

Resolved, 1. That the General Assembly hereby establishes a Standing Committee, to be called "The Church Extension Committee," a majority of whom shall reside in or near the city of Philadelphia. This Committee shall have no other powers than those conferred by the Assembly; and the functions now assigned to them are those of employing Presbyterial, Synodical, and other Presbyterian itinerant or exploring agents, and affording aid in such exceptional cases as those already mentioned, and also the receiving and disbursing of funds for these objects.

2. That, in recommending this course of action, the General Assembly distinctly declare that it is not their intention thus to establish an Ecclesiastical Board, or to interfere with the proper functions of the American Home Missionary Society, but, as heretofore, they recommend that Society to the confidence and coöperation of the churches under their care.

3. That the Standing Committee on Church Extension, now constituted, shall consist of fifteen members, to be chosen by the Assembly in such manner as the Assembly may direct, and the Committee shall, at its first meeting, divide itself into three equal parts, to serve respectively one, two, and three years, but the same persons shall be reëligible at the pleasure of the Assembly.

4. Five members of the Committee shall be a quorum; but in order to elect any salaried officer of the Committee,

or to increase or diminish the salary of the same, a majority of the Committee shall be necessary to constitute a quorum. The Committee shall have power to fill any vacancies occurring while the Assembly is not in session, and they shall make an annual report to the Assembly of all their proceedings.

DECLARATION OF PRINCIPLES.

The following Report was unanimously adopted at a meeting of the Church Extension Committee, held in New York, on Monday, July 23, 1855.

The following Resolutions, passed by the General Assembly, at its meeting in May last, constituted the Committee on Church Extension, and also defined and limited its functions:

"*Resolved*, 1. That the General Assembly hereby establishes a Standing Committee, to be called 'The Church Extension Committee,' a majority of whom shall reside in or near the city of Philadelphia. This Committee shall have no other powers than those conferred by the Assembly; and the functions now assigned to them are those of employing Presbyterial, Synodical, and other Presbyterian itinerant or exploring agents, and affording aid in such exceptional cases as those already mentioned, and also the receiving and disbursing of funds for these objects.

"2. That in recommending this course of action, the General Assembly distinctly declare that it is not their intention thus to establish an Ecclesiastical Board, or to interfere with the proper functions of the American Home Missionary Society, but, as heretofore, they recommend that Society to the confidence and coöperation of the churches under their care."

Three points seem to be plainly involved in these resolutions. 1st, That this Committee is a supplementary agency, and is designed to act in harmony with the A. H. M. S. in the work of home evangelization. 2nd, That its specific object is to perform a certain portion of this great work, which either cannot be done at all, or else cannot be so properly and efficiently done, by the A. H. M. S. 3rd, That in carrying out this design, the Committee is to consider itself as engaged primarily in missionary and not mere ecclesiastical work. In other words, its first and controlling aim, is the extension of the Kingdom of Christ.

Thus far the intention of the Assembly, in the establishment of this Committee, is clear and well-defined. Our exclusive business is to attend to those cases of home missionary effort, which are excluded by the rules or Constitution of the A. H. M. S. That there are such cases, is undeniable. Indeed, in the present posture of our religious affairs, it could not be otherwise. The coöperative principle, upon which the A. H. M. S. is organized, binds that institution to ignore all denominational motive in executing its sacred trust. It is precluded by its Constitution from affording aid to sustain a feeble church, or to plant a new one, because the applicants wish it to be either Presbyterian or Congregational. And yet over the entire field of home missionary effort, the number of Congregationalists, who are unwilling to become Presbyterians, and of Presbyterians, who are unwilling to become Congregationalists, is constantly increasing. While the Plan of Union was in force, this circumstance did not occasion serious embarrassment. But the case is greatly altered now. There are Congregational elements, which, if not gathered into churches of that order, will be scattered among communions not in connection with the A. H. M. S. They will not attach themselves to our branch of the Presbyterian Church. And, on the other hand, there are Presbyterian elements, which, if not gathered into churches of that order, will, in like manner, be lost both to ourselves, and to the A. H. M. S. They will not become Congregationalists. Several well-known causes have for some time been in operation, tending greatly to increase this disposition. We may deeply lament that such a feeling should exist in either of the great Christian bodies, whose coöperation in home and foreign missions God has so signally blessed, and whose relations to each other in former days were so trustful and affectionate; but our lamentation, unfortunately, cannot alter the fact. In this state of things, is it not the part of Christian wisdom to leave that portion of the home mission work, which directly involves these fixed ecclesiastical preferences, to the separate action of the denominations concerned? When either Congregationalists or Presbyterians, with the view of forming a new church of their own order, wish to engage in an enterprise, which the rules of the A. H. M. S. preclude it from aiding, let them be helped by their own denominations, in such a manner as the latter may deem expedient. It certainly appears very plain, that in consequence of the abrogation of the Plan of Union, and other causes already referred to, a considerable department of home missionary labor has of late become so closely involved with denominational interests, that the A. H. M. S. will be able to cultivate it only at the risk of constant suspicion and misunderstanding. Unless in some way such causes of jealousy and irritation be removed, the Society itself must be seriously hindered in its benevolent work. "*For how can two walk,*"—still more, labor—"*together, unless they be agreed?*"

In establishing a Committee on Church-Extension then, the General Assembly was actuated by no unfriendly feeling towards the Society, whose history and noble Christian services reflect such lasting honor upon both Congregationalists and Presbyterians. On the contrary, it warmly recommended that Society, as it had so often before done, to the confidence and coöperation of the churches under its care. But while doing this, it could not turn a deaf ear to the earnest and repeated appeals of its own Synods, Presbyteries, and members. It is bound to listen to such appeals by its very Constitution. Memorials similar to those presented at St. Louis, occupied no small part of its time at Washington, in 1852; and a Committee was then appointed to confer on the matter with the Executive Committee of the A. H. M. S. The subject was again brought forward, and considered with much deliberation, at subsequent meetings of the Assembly.

To meet such appeals in a practical way, without entrenching upon the functions, or diverting money from the treasury of the A. H. M. S., is the object of this Committee. Three distinct functions are assigned to it in the resolution by which it is established.

1st. That of "employing Presbyterial, Synodical, and other Presbyterian itinerant or exploring agents." The employment of such agents, or missionaries, was earnestly recommended by the General Assembly at Washington, in 1852, and it was even hoped that the A. H. M. S. might find itself authorized to sustain them. The suggestion was made in perfect good faith towards that Society, and from a belief that its own interests, as well as those of the Presbyterian Church, would thus be promoted. In the same good faith the Assembly has empowered this Committee to act in the matter. We shall aim so to perform this part of our duty, as not to thwart but to further the home missionary work. And nothing would gratify us more than to see our Congregational brethren doing the same thing. If the two bodies could at once send forth a band of itinerant missionaries of the right stamp—men of single-hearted devotion to Christ, and seeking, first of all, the salvation of souls—to explore, each in his own field, the vast wastes and new settlements of the Northwest, who doubts that the H. M. S., as well as the denominations themselves, would soon have occasion to rejoice in the blessed fruits of such labor? How many scattered sheep in the wilderness would thus be cheered and fed! How many germs of prosperous Christian communities nurtured into strength! It is well known that the agents of the H. M. S. are often not a little perplexed in organizing new churches; for every such church must now be either Presbyterian or Congregational; and how easily are suspicions excited that the agent is biased, and is willing to bias others, in favor of his own ecclesiastical polity! So strongly has this evil been felt, that some of the most devoted and judicious friends of the H. M. S. have counseled that it should abandon altogether the work of exploration to the denominations which sustain it. This work, at any rate, is imperative upon every branch of the body of Christ. Wherever our brethren and sisters are scattered in the wilderness, they should be visited, comforted, fed with the bread of life, and if practicable, organized into churches.

But to obviate all misapprehension, it seems proper to add that this Committee are not authorized to send such missionaries into neighborhoods already adequately supplied with the means of grace.

2nd. Our second function is that of "affording aid in such exceptional cases as those" mentioned in the preamble to the resolutions. Two classes of cases are there designated,(*a*) "The planting of Presbyterian churches in advance of all others in towns and neighborhoods." The phrase "in advance of all others," has been interpreted by some to indicate a purpose of *forestalling* our Congregational brethren; but nothing could be further from the thought of the Assembly. The overtures and memorials upon which its action in this matter was based, stated a variety of cases excluded by the rules of the A. H. M. S., and claiming, as the memorialists urged, the attention of that body, to which, as the general representative council of our Church, its missionary interests are specially entrusted by the Constitution itself. The phrase in question was employed to distinguish and individualize one class of these exceptional cases. It may have been unfortunately chosen; but it had no sinister or sectarian meaning in the intention of the Assembly. Many of our oldest and worthiest members are scattered through the new settlements of the great West; they have pitched their tents in the wilderness or on the prairies of Northern Illinois, Iowa, Wisconsin, and Minnesota; far in advance, perhaps, of all others, they find themselves sufficiently numerous to form a neighborhood, and the nucleus of a flourishing town. With a little aid from abroad, they will soon be able to organize themselves into a church. But they wish it to be Presbyterian; and if the H. M. S. is not yet prepared to assist them, they apply for help to their brethren of the same faith and order. It is the only other source to which they can look. Now to render aid in such a case, is to "plant a Presbyterian church in advance of all others" in this town and neighborhood. The motive is not to keep out other evangelical bodies; it is to forestall evil, and to further the cause of our Redeemer, while, at the same time, we fulfill a solemn duty to our less favored brethren. Once organized, this church may properly apply at once to the A. H. M. S. for aid, and that Society, if there be no good reason to the contrary, would doubtless render it. Cases of this general type are not infrequent, and they are sure to increase among both Presbyterians and Congregationalists, as by means of railroads and steamboats, emigration presses onward at larger and quicker strides into the unoccupied territory of the Northwest. Cases of a somewhat similar character, equally entitled to the attention and liberality of our church, are likely to occur in Tennessee, Mississippi, and other Southern States; cases which the A. H. M. S. would, perhaps, find itself still more embarrassed in meeting. In executing this part of the work assigned us, we feel authorized to disclaim, and do disclaim, both for the Assembly and in our own name, any other design than that of fulfilling a plain Christian duty, in entire good faith towards our Congregational brethren and the H. M. S.

(*b*) The second class of cases, referred to in the resolution, respects "the founding of churches within the chartered limits of cities and large villages." This is, without doubt, the most expensive and important function assigned to the Committee. The A. H. M. S. long since deemed it needful to adopt rules, by which far the larger portion of this work is precluded from the sphere of its operations. Of course, what that Society cannot perform must be done, if at all, by such other instrumentalities as appear best fitted to secure the object in view. The extension of the kingdom of Christ "within the chartered limits of cities and large villages," has become a distinct department of home missionary effort. Under the name of City Missions, it has been carried on, of late years, with unwonted zeal, by all evangelical churches, and is justly regarded by them as as among their most weighty and solemn functions. How to systematize and render more successful this kind of evangelism, is a problem of the first magnitude. In Philadelphia, New York, Newark, and many other Eastern cities, the work has been, and may perhaps best continue to be, done by purely local arrangements; but in the large villages and nascent cities of the West and South, the case is different. The churches there need help from abroad, in sustaining their colonies and new enterprises; and so rapid is the advance of population and wealth, that if thus assisted at the right moment, the infant congregation of to-day often expands, after two or three years, into the mature, self-sustaining church. Solicitations for pecuniary aid in enterprises of this sort, have been so numerous and urgent at the East, that the most liberal have become weary of them. There is a general conviction that such appeals should henceforth be made to a committee authorized to consider and, if deemed best, respond to them. In this way the wealthy members of our churches, as well as pastors and sessions, will be relieved of a distracting burden; the expense, often not small, of special agencies to the East, will be saved, and the same money heretofore contributed, sometimes very much in ignorance or at random, will be far more wisely and systematically disbursed. It cannot be doubted that the result would prove highly favorable, not only to our Church, but also to the interests of the H. M. Society.

It is well known that our Congregational brethren in New England and elsewhere, have, in various ways, responded to similar appeals from the West; and that, too, without diminishing at all their generous contributions to the H. M. Society. We cannot believe that they will blame us for doing the same thing in such a mode as seems to us best fitted to promote the cause of our One Lord and Redeemer.

3rd. The last function assigned to this Committee is that of "receiving and disbursing funds," for the objects already mentioned. How large an amount of funds will be needed to meet the exceptional cases, that may properly claim our help, cannot, of course, be predetermined. But, for some time, it will not probably exceed what has been annually contributed to similar objects in our Church, by means of correspondence, personal solicitations, and special agencies. We have no wish to divert collections from the treasury of the H. M. S.; on the contrary, we hope and expect that this supplementary agency, by increasing light, quickening the sense of Christian duty, and exciting fresh zeal among our people, in relation to the vast work of home evangelization, as also by adding to the number of giving churches, will tend, both directly and indirectly, to enhance the receipts of that Society. We shall be sadly disappointed at a contrary result.

Such is a brief statement of the design of the General Assembly in establishing this Committee, and of the principles by which we intend to be governed in performing the duties assigned us. We feel quite sure that the end of our appointment will be most fully accomplished by preserving, if possible, unharmed, the holy ties of fraternal confidence and love, which have so long united us and our Congregational brethren in furthering, at home and over all the earth, the kingdom of our Blessed Lord. We are not insensible that the work entrusted to us is beset with some difficulties, and cannot be rightly done without wisdom from above. That we, together with our whole Church, may be largely replenished with this inestimable grace, and that all our action may be "*first pure, then peaceable, gentle, easy to be entreated, full of mercy and good fruits, without partiality and without hypocrisy,*" is our sincere wish and shall be our constant prayer.

RULES.

I. Quarterly meetings of the Committee shall be held alternately in the cities of Philadelphia and New York, on the third Tuesdays of April, July, October, and January, at one o'clock P. M., at which meetings alone the more important business not requiring haste shall be transacted; such as the appointing of officers, determining the policy of the Committee, adopting rules or changing them, and agreeing upon the Annual Report to the General Assembly. Beside the quarterly meetings there shall be held monthly meetings, excepting in those months in which the quarterly meetings occur, at the Presbyterian House in Philadelphia, at which meetings all ordinary executive business not reserved as above, may be transacted. The chairman may convene the Committee at any other time by causing suitable notice to be given. The necessary travelling expenses of the ministerial members of the Committee shall be paid by the Treasurer.

II. A Secretary and a Treasurer shall be chosen annually, by nomination and ballot.

III. While the Secretary shall be careful not to interfere with the collections made for the American Home Missionary Society or its auxiliaries, yet it is understood that the claims of the Committee are to be so presented to individuals and churches, as to secure adequate funds to carry ont all the objects designed by the General Assembly in its appointment.

IV. The ordinary mode of operation of the Committee will be through the Synods or Presbyteries of our Church, upon the following plan: Each Synod or Presbytery which thinks proper to do so may appoint a Committee on Church Extension, where such a Committee does not already exist, composed of members so situated that they can readily meet. When cases occur such as come within the range of our appointment, the Synodical or Presbyterial Committee will recommend the field, or church, or minister, as the case may be, and in general coöperate with this Committee in regard to this class of domestic missionary operations. It will be understood, however, in cases where the Synod or Presbytery has not acted, that churches or ministers may address the Committee directly.

V. Synods or Presbyteries coöperating with the Committee will either send to it all their funds collected for the class of cases appropriate to the Committee, and the appointments be made by it; or they may raise their own funds and make appointments to be confirmed by this Committee, and pay over to it their surplus.

VI. Applications should always be specific. They should state such particulars as the following: The circumstances which make the case one proper for the action of this Committee and not for that of the American Home Missionary Society; the extent and location of the field; the name of the agent or missionary; if a church or congregation, its name and location; the number of communicants; the average number of attendants on public worship; the state of the country and population, and prospects of the field; the denominations and size of congregations immediately contiguous; the total amount of salary which they can raise for the given time, or which can be raised in the Synod or Presbytery, and every other particular calculated to throw light upon the case.

VII. All coöperating Committees will make an annual report to the Committee, and all agents or missionaries receiving from it the whole or a part of their support, will make a quarterly report. The annual reports shall be forwarded in time to be received by the second Tuesday of April, in each year, and the quarterly reports by the second Tuesdays of July, October, and January.

ADDRESS.

TO THE MINISTERS, RULING ELDERS, AND MEMBERS OF THE PRESBYTERIAN CHURCH.

DEAR BRETHREN:—

We have some fears that you may not apprehend the extent of the claims upon our Church Extension Committee. It is intended to systematize all those applications which have been heretofore made to individuals and churches, for assistance in the support of ministers of our Church, whether as pastors, as missionaries engaged in establishing one or more churches, or as exploring agents itinerating through the limits of a Synod or a State, except in those cases already met by the coöperative missionary societies. It will be readily seen that the cases must be very numerous in which, without interfering with other denominations, we shall be called to extend aid. Every Presbyterian church and minister has a special claim on us. We are not a local committee, originated by a city or neighborhood, or by a presbytery or synod. The entire Church is to look to us, and that exploration which is appropriate to a separate denomination, so far as our Church is concerned, we are to be prepared to accomplish; whether in the vast West or South, or in the immense unoccupied wastes of California and Oregon. New churches planted in cities and towns, where the rules of the American Home Missionary Society forbid their acting, will come upon us in numbers and involving much expense.

Whoever has imagined that the Assembly in appointing this Committee has undertaken a slight work, has very much misapprehended the case. It will not do for a Church like ours to loiter behind their brethren in filling this land with the Gospel. We do not desire, indeed, to stimulate you to sectarian ambition, but we do wish that you may be enterprising in that high and holy sense which places Christ and His cause before all things in your estimation. What the Committee can do, depends upon yourselves. We are the almoners of the Church. If your spirit is contracted, so must our appropriations be, and if the harvest perish on the field, after every appeal made by us, you, dear brethren, will be responsible. A healthful activity is essential to the very existence of a Church like ours.

The idea which we would impress upon you, if we could, is, that this is a work belonging to the whole body in common. Every church should do something for it. It is not a want that can be met by a few hundred dollars from a few individuals in the large cities. It is one which will involve the expenditure of thousands, and the means to meet it must be gathered wherever there is a hand to help, or a heart to beat for true religion, or to feel for our brethren scattered through the wilderness. If you will look at the magnitude of the work, we are sure that you will not fail to supply the means.

We are aware that the peculiar position of our Church necessitates, at this time, a large expenditure for other objects. We would be very far from wishing to interfere with these. But, brethren, is it not a privilege to labor and to give for Christ, and is it not a glorious thing to belong to a Church like ours which stands for truth and freedom, and which rises with the greatness of the occasion to meet every responsibility? The weak are crushed by such accumulated responsibilities, but the strong bear them up, sustained by the right arm of the Mightiest, and gain strength by endurance and by exercise. We welcome you to constant toil and generous exertion until this whole land and the world shall be given to Christ, and presently, we trust, we shall all be welcomed to the faithful laborer's rest and to the victor's crown.

As the Committee have, at present, no officer who can visit the churches and make personal application to them, we must rely upon the officers and members of the churches themselves, and in order to make our appeal more definite, the Committee have appointed the *second Sabbath of November*, for a simultaneous collection throughout our whole Church for this object. We earnestly appeal to every minister and church not to disregard this appointment. If the collection be even small, let it be given with a good will and with fervent prayer to the Great Head of the Church for His blessing upon our efforts.

ALBERT BARNES,
THOMAS J. SHEPHERD,
BENJAMIN J. WALLACE,
JOHN A. BROWN,
GEORGE L. PRENTISS,
SAMUEL T. SPEAR,
JOHN L. MASON,
THOMAS BRAINERD,
HENRY DARLING,
MATTHEW W. BALDWIN,
THOMAS P. SPARHAWK,
JONATHAN F. STEARNS,
JOHN C. SMITH,
JOSEPH B. SHEFFIELD,
EDWARD A. LAMBERT.

www.ingramcontent.com/pod-product-compliance
Lightning Source LLC
LaVergne TN
LVHW020639110826
845149LV00004B/1285

* 9 7 8 1 4 1 8 1 9 0 5 1 4 *